THE ACA LEGAL SERIES
Volume 5

"THE COUNSELOR AS EXPERT WITNESS"

THE ACA LEGAL SERIES

Series Editor: Theodore P. Remley, Jr., JD, PhD

Volume 1   **Preparing for Court Appearances**
Theodore P. Remley, Jr., JD, PhD

Volume 2   **Documentation in Counseling Records**
Robert W. Mitchell, ACSW

Volume 3   **Law and Management of a Counseling Agency or Private Practice**
Ronald K. Bullis, MDiv, JD

Volume 4   **Counseling Minor Clients**
Mark M. Salo, MEd
Stephen G. Shumate, JD, MS

Volume 5   **The Counselor as Expert Witness**
William J. Weikel, PhD
Paula Richardson Hughes, JD

Volume 6   **Confidentiality and Privileged Communication**
Gibbs L. Arthur, Jr., MEd
Carl D. Swanson, JD, EdD

Volume 7   **Legal Issues in Marriage and Family Counseling**
Patricia Stevens-Smith, PhD
Marcia M. Hughes, JD

THE ACA LEGAL SERIES
Volume 5

"THE COUNSELOR AS EXPERT WITNESS"

William J. Weikel, PhD
Paula Richardson Hughes, JD

Series Editor
Theodore P. Remley, Jr., JD, PhD

Copyright © 1993 by the American Counseling Association

All rights reserved.

American Counseling Association
5999 Stevenson Avenue
Alexandria, VA 22304

Cover design by Sarah Jane Valdez

Library of Congress Cataloging-in-Publication Data

Weikel, William J.
   The counselor as expert witness / William J. Weikel, Paula Richardson Hughes.
     p. cm. — (The ACA legal series ; v. 5)
   Includes bibliographical references.
   ISBN 1-55620-106-0
   1. Evidence, Expert—United States. 2. Psychology, Forensic—United States. 3. Confidential communications—United States. I. Hughes, Paula Richardson. II. Title. III. Series.
KF8965.W45 1993
347.73067—dc20
[347.30767]
                                                                                    92-32731
                                                                                                     CIP

The ACA Legal Series, Volume 5

Printed in the United States of America

To the memory of my father, Ellsworth E. Weikel, 1912–1991.
William J. Weikel

To my father, Judge James M. Richardson, who epitomizes what an attorney should be—an honest, intelligent, caring person with good common sense.
Paula Richardson Hughes

Contents

Biographies	ix
Preface	1
Glossary	3
When Should an Expert Be Used?	7
Agreeing to Serve as an Expert Witness	11
Types of Actions	17
Relationships With Parties Being Evaluated	27
The Attorney's Role	31
Preparing to Testify and Giving Testimony	37
Frequently Asked Questions	43
Guidelines for Practice	47
Summary	49
Discussion Questions	51
Suggested Readings	53
References	55

Biographies

William J. Weikel is a professor and chair of the Department of Leadership and Secondary Education at Morehead State University in Kentucky. Dr. Weikel has served as a contract vocational expert for the Office of Hearings and Appeals of the Social Security Administration since 1976. He has also been in private practice, specializing in providing expert witness testimony since 1983. Dr. Weikel has "taken the oath" for depositions, administrative law hearings, civil suits, federal tort suits and various other actions several thousand times. He received his PhD in counselor education with a minor in rehabilitation from the University of Florida in Gainesville. His master of arts was in rehabilitation counseling from the University of Scranton, Pennsylvania. Dr. Weikel is a past president of the American Mental Health Counselors Association (AMHCA) and has chaired the American Counseling Association's (ACA) Government Relations Committee and Strategic Planning Committee. He is also a past Kentucky Association for Counseling and Development president and chair of the Southern Region of ACA. Dr. Weikel is a National Certified Counselor, a Certified Clinical Mental Health Counselor, and a diplomate with the American Board of Vocational Experts. He is the father of two children.

Paula Richardson Hughes is a 1978 graduate of Morehead State University and a 1980 graduate of the University of Kentucky College of Law. She has been licensed to practice law in Kentucky since 1981, where she is a member of the Kentucky

Bar Association and the Kentucky Academy of Trial Attorneys. She is also a member of the American Bar Association and the American Trial Lawyers Association. Although the state of Kentucky does not allow specialization in the practice of law, Ms. Hughes' practice is concentrated in the areas of personal injury and Workers' Compensation. She has extensive trial experience and has deposed "more experts than she wants to count." Ms. Hughes is married and the mother of three children.

Theodore P. Remley, Jr., Series Editor, is Executive Director of the American Counseling Association. Immediately prior to assuming this position, Dr. Remley was chair of the Department of Counselor Education at Mississippi State University in Starkville. He holds a PhD from the Department of Counselor Education at the University of Florida in Gainesville and a JD in law from the Catholic University of America in Washington, DC.

Preface

The words "Do you swear to tell the truth and the whole truth, so help you God?" and "I do" are spoken, and the adrenalin begins to flow! Serving as an expert witness in various legal actions is perhaps the epitome of excitement for a mental health professional. By qualifying as an expert witness and agreeing to serve, you are consenting to share your specialized knowledge and opinions with judges or juries who must make difficult yet informed decisions. Your role is to convey your knowledge to these noncounselors in an unbiased, objective fashion, without allowing the formality of the proceedings, or the jargon, to interfere with your testimony.

The rules regarding confidentiality and client advocacy change when you assume the role of an expert witness. Now, rather than keeping interactions confidential, you are expected to convey what you know about a specific problem, or what you have discovered about a particular person. Often you have examined or tested someone for the specific purpose of sharing those findings with the court, or to help you develop and render a professional opinion. In these instances, you must make it clear to the client that confidentiality is not in effect. What you learn about that individual through interviewing and testing is for the specific purpose of helping the courts make an informed decision. Clients must be advised plainly and clearly of your role before any face-to-face interaction occurs.

In most actions, you are subject to questioning by attorneys representing the clients involved. You need to know what to expect in terms of the questions posed to you and the procedures to be employed as the attorneys examine, cross-examine, redirect, and re-cross. You are likely to have to produce your notes, files, and possibly even actual tests concerning the client, if testing was conducted.

In this monograph, we share with you our knowledge and experiences—as a counselor with extensive expert witness experience and as a trial attorney who regularly utilizes expert witnesses from a variety of disciplines. This information, coupled with the knowledge you have gained from the other monographs in this series, will allow you to decide whether or not the challenging role of expert witness is for you. If you decide in the affirmative, you will have the basic knowledge of the process, procedures, and ethical issues to allow you to function efficiently in this exciting role!

Glossary

Adversarial Testimony: Testimony that is offered on behalf of and by one party to further that party's claim against an opposing party.

Child Custody Case: A civil litigation in which a court decides who will have physical custody of children. Usually a parent is granted custody, but not always. A grandparent, other relative, or court-appointed custodian are also among those who may be granted custody.

Competency Hearing: A trial in which a judge or jury decides whether an individual has the physical and mental capacity to manage his or her personal affairs.

Contingency Fee: A contract arrangement in which the compensation to be paid for a service is a percentage of the final settlement or award. Attorneys typically work on a contingency basis; experts should not.

Cross-examination: The questioning of the witness by the attorney of the opposing party after the direct examination.

Defendant: An individual or entity against whom a claim is brought.

Deposition: A sworn statement given before a court reporter outside the court setting. In a deposition, the opposing counsel has the opportunity to discover what you plan to testify to at a later date or at trial. Depositions are sometimes taken in lieu of your appearance at a trial. In these instances, you will be questioned and cross-examined as if you were in court, and a transcription of the proceedings will be read into evidence at the actual trial, just as if you were there to testify in person. Some jurisdictions now allow video depositions in place of live testimony. These are taken beforehand and then actually shown to the judge or jury at the trial.

Direct Examination: The questioning of a witness by the attorney who called the person as a witness.

Dual Relationship: A relationship in which a professional knows a subject in more than one capacity. An example is a counselor educator who has an individual as a graduate student and agrees to see that student as a client in his or her counseling practice while that person is still a student. Counselors are admonished by their ethical code to avoid dual relationships.

Expert Witness: An individual who is qualified by education and experience to give an opinion in his or her field that is beyond the knowledge of the ordinary layperson. An example is a mental health counselor's testimony/opinion on a person's parenting skills in relation to custody proceedings.

Impeachment: Questioning the veracity of the witness by means of evidence offered for that purpose or by raising the possibility that the witness is not to be believed.

Litigation: The process that follows the filing a claim. Litigation includes defending a claim, the discovery process, the actual hearing or trial, and the appeals process beyond the verdict or judgment.

Malpractice: The commission of a negligent act by a professional in the performance of his or her profession.

On Record: This term describes the periods during a proceeding that are being recorded by a tape-recording device or on a stenographic machine by a court reporter or notary public. These recordings, which are made, for example, during the questions and answers of a deposition and conversations among the attorneys, are transcribed into typewritten pages and used as evidence in the claim.

Plaintiff: An individual or entity who initiates litigation against a defendant.

Prior Knowledge: Previous information regarding a specific client or case. In most cases, you will not be able to appear as an expert or objective witness if you have prior knowledge.

Res Judicata: A matter that has already been decided or adjudged.

Subpoena: A court document served upon an individual or entity to appear at a proceeding for the purpose of giving testimony.

Vocational Expert: An individual who is qualified by education and experience to give testimony concerning an individual's occupational disability or lost future earnings potential.

Voir Dire: Questioning an expert witness concerning his or her qualifications or expertise in a particular area. Voir dire is also an examination by the court or attorneys of prospective jurors to determine their qualifications to serve on a jury.

When Should an Expert Be Used?

Probably the better question is "When should an expert not be used?" Litigation has become more complex, so attorneys have become more likely to use experts to help prove their cases before judges and juries. In some types of cases, the use of an expert is a foregone conclusion. For example, a medical doctor is necessary in proving that injuries occurred and that a person has suffered pain from those injuries.

In the past, no witness, not even a qualified expert, was allowed to testify as to the ultimate fact the jury or judge was to decide, for example, as to whether one spouse has been psychologically abusing the other or as to the amount of future wages a worker will not earn because he or she can no longer perform the past work due to injuries. Legally, the determining factor as to whether a competent, qualified, expert's opinion is admissible, is whether the opinion assists rather than impedes a judge or the jury in resolving the issues of the case. The judge presiding over the case decides whether an expert opinion is admissible. If the opposing counsel does not raise the question, the opinion is admitted.

Attorneys should look at each case and ask the question, "Will this expert's opinion tip the scales in my client's favor?" Frequently, the answer is "Yes."

Once the determination has been made to use expert testimony in a particular case, the attorney must select the best person to testify. In practice, the best sources for finding experts are other attorneys. There are also several private companies that advertise experts for hire. Most attorneys will tell you that they are inundated with mailings from these "experts for hire," and many report that they have not had great success with this particular method of selection.

Selection of an expert often depends upon the type of testimony to be given: in person before a jury or in a sworn, written deposition testimony for an administrative law judge. As a potential expert witness, you should know whether the testimony is for a jury or for an administrative law judge because it may make a difference in how you should prepare.

The judge determines whether an individual qualifies as a competent expert in a given field. The attorney who retains you, for whose client you have been hired to testify, asks specific questions to show the court that you are a qualified expert in the field. If the case is not before a jury, do not be surprised if very little time is spent on your qualifications. If you are testifying in a Workers' Compensation case as a vocational expert, for example, the attorney is taking testimony by deposition and is looking for any way to shorten the deposition to save time and money.

If you are called as an expert witness *for* one side, you are automatically testifying *against* the other parties. Most attorneys want a pleasant, knowledgeable person as an expert witness. Playing hardball and being aggressive turns off the judge or the jury. However, the expert must be firm in his or her opinion. We have seen various experts say one thing in a pretrial conference, then waiver and weaken their testimony in cross-examination. Therefore, state your opinion firmly, explain it if necessary, and do not waiver. Furthermore, do not drone on and on. Pontificating bores the jury and guarantees that the attorney will not hire you in the future.

One of the things you must remember is that experts can only give opinions on subjects for which they are qualified. If attorneys ask you to give an opinion that you do not feel qualified to give, tell them so. Opposing attorneys on cross-examination may attempt to draw the expert out of his or her field to jeopardize the previous qualified opinions the expert has given. Politely tell the opposing attorney, "I am not qualified to give such an opinion." When experts venture outside of their realm of expertise, they become a liability to the case rather than an asset.

There are situations in which experts should not be used. Unfortunately, the question of whether to use an expert is usually one of hindsight—and that is always 20/20.

If you want to testify regularly as an expert witness, you must establish a network of contacts. That means marketing yourself as an expert. Always have your cards available and give them to all attorneys. Be willing to speak to local and state bar associations and trial attorneys at their meetings. Use social gatherings to meet potential employers. Consider sending a professional announcement (following ethical guidelines) highlighting this aspect of your practice to local attorneys and judges. Find out which local, state, and federal agencies have expertise in your area and meet with them to discuss a contractual arrangement. Your best source of future referrals are the attorneys representing the "other side" in a present case.

A word of caution: As an expert, you are only as good as your reputation for honesty. Never hedge or give a false opinion even for an attorney you have worked with regularly. An ethical attorney will respect you for this position and continue to use you as an expert.

Agreeing to Serve as an Expert Witness

The initial contact inquiring about your willingness to serve as a possible expert can come in many ways. Typically, an attorney calls you in person, at least for the initial contact, to discuss the case and to give you the overall details. The typical inquiry is "I'm wondering, can you help me in this case?" It should be taken as meaning, "Can your expertise help me inform the judge or jury regarding my client or the issues at question in this case and help them reach an enlightened decision?" It is important to stress that your testimony is for the purpose of assisting a judge or jury to make a decision in a case and not for helping the plaintiff or defendant to win. After the initial contact or first few times you work with a particular attorney or court, you are most likely to receive calls directly from an attorney's secretary, assistant, or paralegal to inquire about your availability to evaluate a client or to study another case. Part of your decision-making process should include the ethical question, "Do I have the necessary knowledge and skills by virtue of my education and training to provide the requested services?" Next you must ask yourself, "Do I possess the personality traits and have the self-skills that will allow me to perform in a professional manner in this potentially stressful situation?" If your answers to the above questions are "Yes," and you can make the commitment in terms of time, you can agree to provide services in a fair and objective manner. If you lack any of these traits and skills or have any conflict of interest, such as having a prior knowledge of the case, having a dual relationship with one of the principals, or standing to gain in any way from the outcome of the case, then your answer must be "No."

In other actions, such as Social Security Disability hearings or child custody cases, you may have an ongoing contract to provide expert testimony directly to the courts. In such instances, you have a continuing relationship with the appropriate agency, and the agency simply inquires regarding your availability to serve on various dates at prearranged or set rates. Remley and Miranti (1991) noted the increasing use of mental health counselors as evaluators in child custody cases to make an impartial recommendation to a judge regarding a child's best interests in a custody decision. Earlier, Weikel and Palmo (1989) advocated this role for mental health counselors, although Gardner (1982) strongly suggested that counselors accept this role only as appointed by the courts and not as an advocate for either side. Both parties then share in paying the counselor's fee. Likewise, you may be invited by the court to submit your credentials to serve on a roster of mental health professionals available for various other actions in which impartial testimony is deemed helpful. Again, you must examine the docket or schedule of cases to determine if you have any prior knowledge or conflict of interest that might cause you to disqualify yourself. Your impartiality is critical! You are and must be an impartial expert, not a client advocate or champion for any particular cause. Therefore, it is incumbent upon you to disqualify yourself in any case where you have prior knowledge that may cloud your objectivity or if you could enjoy personal gain depending upon the outcome of a case. Not to decline serving in inappropriate cases is a serious ethical violation with possible legal ramifications.

In the initial contact, the attorney or agency who retains you is likely to inquire about fees. Most counselors charge their full hourly rate for all preliminary matters, such as studying a case, attorney conferences, interviewing a client, or testing. These fees should be in line with what counselors and related mental health professionals in your geographic region are currently charging. If you are requested to prepare a written report or opinion, this too should be at your typical hourly fee. With a little experience, you should be able to give prospective employers an accurate estimate regarding time and cost for most cases. For example, the authors have found that a "typical" Workers' Compensation case takes about 3 hours from the initial contact through the written report stage. Giving an accurate cost estimate to attorneys who inquire can help them decide whether or not to retain you. You also need to discuss when payment is expected. We suggest that a bill be sent when services are provided and that you convey to retaining attorneys that you expect prompt payment, that is, within 30 to 90 days. Various state, federal and local agencies and courts have you submit itemized bills or vouchers and pay as per their usual custom, which, in our experience, is usually within 45 to 90 days. Many experts have followed the practice of the legal profession and require a retainer or advance payment. This is a personal decision for you to make.

Fees for depositions vary greatly even among the same profession, possibly because many professionals are threatened by this intensive questioning of their findings and keep their prices high to avoid being deposed. Most, however, charge from two to four times their regular hourly rate with a minimum 1 hour charge. This allows for case preparation and review of notes, an attorney conference prior to the deposition, and time for all parties to arrive and get ready to begin. Most charge extra if travel is involved. For instance, a counselor who charges $75 per hour for counseling or other professional services might charge $250 per hour, 1 hour minimum, for a deposition and $1,000 per day for an appearance "live" at a trial or hearing. In our experience, these fees are not out of line with what other mental health professionals are charging and are downright bargains compared to what experts in certain fields demand! Under no circumstance may an expert witness accept a case on a contingency fee basis! This means that your fees must be set in advance and are in no way dependent on the outcome of the case. Your fee structure should be the same regardless of who retains you—the plaintiff or the defense—and must be consistent from case to case. The only exception is when you have an ongoing contract with some agency or court jurisdiction for a preagreed, set fee, consistent with the customary rate. Remember, all you—like any attorney—have to offer is your time, knowledge, and expertise, and bill accordingly.

On rare occasions, you may be asked to see a client to provide counseling services after your involvement as an expert witness has ceased. In our opinion, this is ethical, provided the legal proceedings and your involvement in them have ended. The client must be advised that once you have agreed to provide traditional counseling services, you, as a professional, have forfeited your right to serve that client as an impartial expert should there be any future action or litigation. Once again, this is necessary to avoid a potential dual relationship. Some authors disagree with us and say that you should decline to provide counseling services to a client with whom you have been involved as an expert witness. However, our position remains that if clear lines are drawn between the roles and you don't try to "flip flop" between roles, there is no ethical violation. It is also appropriate at this point to employ whatever fee structure you typically employ in providing your counseling services. Remember, in the event that you are called upon to provide future expert witness services for this client, you must disqualify yourself because you have entered into a new relationship as client advocate and have sacrificed your impartiality.

You will find that private attorneys can be a major referral source for work as an expert. Your relationship with them should be cordial but professional. So too should be your relationship with officers of the court and agency representatives. Never imply that you can "help" them in any way other than as an objective expert. Hired guns who say what an attorney wants them to say are soon run out of Dodge City, and their careers as experts are notably short-lived! You can perform "favors" such as agreeing to see a client on short notice or after traditional hours, or in expediting a report to help an attorney meet his or her proof deadline. However, we cannot stress enough the importance of maintaining the stance of impartial, objective witness. This holds true whether you have worked for an attorney or agency once or a hundred times.

Because there are, for the most part, no guidelines, licenses, or certifications dictating who may serve as an expert witness, per se, it is left up to the presiding judge or hearing officer to decide whether a potential witness qualifies or how much weight to accord his or her testimony. As a potential expert, you will be asked to provide a current curriculum vitae or resume. The resume should include your educational background, membership in professional societies, publications, relevant experience, licenses, and certifications. In many routine proceedings where you are known to the court and attorneys and a jury is not involved, your resume is typed into the record in question-and-answer form as if you had presented it orally. You are likely to be asked on record (under oath or affirmation) to summarize your credentials. You may have to answer specific questions regarding your education, training, or experience. These may be posed by either or both sides' attorneys or the presiding judge or officer. Expect the opposing counselor to voir dire or question because he or she represents the other side in the matter at hand. Opposing counsel may even object to your qualifications as an expert, but the presiding officer makes the ultimate decision. Only rarely have we seen an expert not qualify.

If for any reason you fail to qualify in a particular action, simply compute your fee and send a bill for your services to that point. Anything can happen in court proceedings and often does! Just remember, never guarantee a lawyer that you can qualify as an expert because there are no guarantees in this business. Once you have been acknowledged as an expert, you may respond to questions and render your opinion as asked (Remley, 1991).

Although we have seen experts spend up to 2 hours answering questions regarding their qualifications—degrees, experience, prior testimony, ratio of defense to plaintiff testimony, research, writing, teaching duties, annual salary, salary breakdown—it is more typical that the attorneys are familiar with their work or that the presiding judge has seen them in this court before, and there is, at most, a cursory examination of their credentials. Frequently, well-qualified and experienced experts receive little or no questioning from opposing counsel because the attorney does not want to impress a judge or jury with the expert's often long list of lofty credentials.

Usually, opposing counsel has been provided with an opportunity to examine an expert's vita, and he or she stipulates or agrees that the highlights of the resume can be typed into the transcript of a deposition as if the expert had responded to them in question-and-answer form. Once there is agreement over the qualifications of an expert witness, the proceedings can begin. It is important to remember that you typically are qualified within a specific context and should answer questions only within that role. For example, if you have been retained to give an opinion regarding child custody, you should refrain from giving an opinion, even if trained to do so, regarding the validity of a child's IQ scores as measured by a school psychologist. Knowledgeable and experienced experts stick to their narrowly defined and stipulated area of expertise and defer to other acknowledged experts for opinions outside their defined area.

# Types of Actions

As counselors we have a unique perspective by virtue of our education and training. Part of our uniqueness lies in our psychoeducational orientation and the emphasis we place on prevention. We have concrete skills, and among our ranks are individuals with expertise in individual and group counseling, human assessment, human development, stress management, rehabilitation, addiction, vocational and career development, placement, women's issues, sexual and relationship issues, and child abuse and neglect. As the public and members of other professions recognize the varied expertise in our profession, we can expect increasing numbers of requests to share this knowledge and expertise with the courts. Some of the areas in which professional counselors can be of service as expert witnesses are child custody, divorce, child abuse and neglect, delinquency, the ability to work, sexual harassment, competency, negligence/malpractice, pain and suffering, and addiction.

Child Custody

In certain cases, attorneys or the courts may request a counselor or other mental health professional, such as a child psychologist, social worker, or psychiatrist, to render an opinion regarding custodial issues. The professional is usually requested to interview the child, parent(s), or family to help him or her to render an opinion but, on rare occasions, may be asked to render an opinion on the evidence of record, that is, the findings of other professionals. If an interview takes place, it is without the usual confidential relationship because the findings of the professional are to be shared with the court. Notes, records, and test data are all subject to examination, possibly in open court, because decisions regarding the child's welfare are at stake. The counselor serving in this capacity should have considerable expertise in dealing with children as well as knowledge of child development and family dynamics. A working knowledge of current research regarding child welfare and custody is desirable. As an expert witness, you should be providing friendly (versus adversarial) testimony (Gardner, 1982). That is, you are not an advocate for either parent, but are providing an objective opinion based on your knowledge of the case. Any personal bias disqualifies you from serving in this capacity. See Remley and Miranti (1991) for further guidelines in this area.

These are the kinds of questions expert witnesses involved in child custody cases might be asked:

1. Which parent do you recommend that the child be placed with?
2. Why do you recommend this placement?
3. Assuming that Mr. Jones makes $20,000 more per year than Ms. Jones, don't you think that Mr. Jones can provide more for the child than Ms. Jones? Wouldn't that be a better placement?
4. Do you feel that the child will be in any danger if he or she continued to live with this parent?
5. What psychological theories or assessment instruments have you used in formulating your recommendation?

Divorce

Marriage or family counselors or others could be called upon to serve as experts in many different areas of divorce proceedings. A counselor may be called upon to testify regarding the effects of physical or psychological abuse on a spouse or family. A counselor may also be called upon to testify regarding the educational or training needs of a spouse to become self-sufficient, or to give the earnings capacity of a spouse as projected in the *Occupational Outlook Handbook* or other source documents when there are issues centered around finances to be resolved.

Just as in other actions in which you may be retained by either party, your testimony must be as an impartial expert. You may or may not have had the opportunity for a face-to-face interview with the parties involved, or you may have had several face-to-face sessions along with the opportunity for testing.

These are the kinds of questions expert witnesses involved in divorce cases might be asked:

1. In determining whether or not Mr. or Ms. Jones should receive maintenance payments for a set period, have you determined his or her current income potential?
2. From what you have learned in this case, do you believe that Mr. or Ms. Jones has suffered any psychological abuse from his or her spouse?
3. How serious is the psychological damage or trauma that the client has incurred?
4. What are the long-term effects of psychological and physical abuse on an individual?
5. Has this individual exhibited the characteristics of posttraumatic stress disorder?

Child Abuse and Neglect

School counselors and others may be called upon to serve as what Remley (1991) called *general witnesses*, that is, to provide factual information in cases of child abuse or neglect, but other counselors may serve as expert witnesses. As an expert, you may have examined the child or parties involved and are expected to render an opinion to help the courts make decisions regarding the child's welfare. The expert might appear in custodial, civil, or criminal proceedings.

Although a treating counselor is likely to receive a subpoena to appear in an abuse or neglect case, and should follow the recommendations outlined by Remley (1991) in the first monograph in this series, the expert is retained for a voluntary appearance. The expert may answer specific questions regarding the effects of abuse or neglect or various hypothetical questions as constructed by the attorneys. Your responses to all questions should be based on your knowledge and experience as well as accepted research in the field. Provide specific answers to questions and avoid globalisms or generalities. If you do not know or cannot answer a question as posed in these or any other cases, say so!

These are the kinds of questions expert witnesses involved in child abuse and neglect cases might be asked:

1. How long have you worked with this child and in what capacity?
2. What specific indications of abuse and neglect have you observed?
3. In your opinion, is the child in any psychological or physical danger if he or she remains in this setting?
4. In your opinion, how long has this abuse been taking place?
5. How damaging has this abuse been to the child?
6. Is it your recommendation that this child remain with this parent?

Delinquency

The adjudication of delinquent behavior, an area formerly dominated by social workers, is now more open for input and testimony from counselors, frequently as court-appointed experts. A strong background in child and adolescent development is necessary, as is information regarding the efficacy of various treatment programs. As in other actions, the decisions made in delinquency hearings can be vital, even life or death. An appropriate placement for treatment, versus incarceration or other forms of "punishment," can change the course of a young life. The expert must be well qualified to serve in the best interests of the child or adolescent. Courts are especially likely to accept the recommendations of experts in these and other cases involving the welfare of children.

These are the kinds of questions expert witnesses involved in delinquency cases might be asked:

1. In your opinion, could this child benefit from a residential treatment program at the XYZ Center?
2. Is the treatment provided by the XYZ Center the least restrictive, appropriate treatment available?
3. In your opinion, has this individual's family background contributed to a delinquent situation?
4. Upon what theories or information have you based your recommendation?

The Ability to Work

Workers' Compensation, Social Security Disability Insurance, Supplemental Security Income, personal injury, and negligence are all examples of legal proceedings in which counselors or rehabilitation professionals may be called upon to render an expert opinion regarding an individual's ability to work, the transferable work skills, or loss of wages. Depending upon the specific action, the counselor may interview and test the client, or render an opinion based on the evidence of a written record. Counselors may be asked whether or not an occupational disability exists, based upon some physical or psychological impairment, or how a combination of impairments will affect an individual's ability to work. They may be asked to provide a specific percentage of occupational disability for different scenarios via hypothetical questioning or to discuss a client's loss of income due to a disabling condition. Such an expert, usually called a *vocational expert*, a title derived from a consulting position created by the Office of Hearings and Appeals of the Social Security Administration, should have expertise in vocational matters, such as job demands and job analysis. A working knowledge of medical terminology, psychological terminology, and the vocational implications of various conditions is also necessary. The vocational expert should be versed in employment practices, economic and salary data, and the availability or existence of jobs in the regional and national economy. More recently, vocational experts are entering into economic areas, such as loss of wages and income. Frequently, the expert works in conjunction with an economist who projects present earnings into potential future loss. In cases of wrongful or negligent death, the vocational witness may present data regarding work-life expectancy and present income capacity, based on accepted available data. Factors such as a client's age, education, training, work experience, and physical or mental capacity may all be considered by the expert in reaching an opinion. The expert is not a decider of fact but rather responds to questions, or hypothetical questions, as posed by an attorney, judge, or hearings officer. See Weikel (1986) for more information regarding the counselor as vocational expert witness.

These are the kinds of questions expert witnesses involved in ability-to-work cases might be asked:

1. What medical and psychological reports have you relied on in reaching your opinions?
2. Assuming that Dr. Smith has limited Mr. Jones to lifting no more that 25 pounds frequently and 50 pounds maximum, can he be expected to perform his customary work?
3. Will any special (employer or work) accommodations be necessary for Mr. Jones to perform his job, assuming that the restrictions placed on him by Dr. Smith are correct?
4. What percentage of occupational disability, if any, has Mr. Jones experienced, assuming that the report of Dr. Smith and the restrictions placed on Mr. Jones in that report are correct?
5. Have all of the answers that you've given here today been given within a reasonable degree of vocational probability?

Sexual Harassment

Can anyone who watched the Clarence Thomas/Anita Hill Supreme Court confirmation hearings not question the potential damage and resultant litigation that is possible in cases of sexual harassment? Although this is a relatively new area of litigation, counselors and others with expertise in stress management, employment issues, human development, and gender issues can expect work to emerge for expert witnesses as awareness of the problem spreads. With increased awareness will come an increasing body of knowledge and the need for experts to interpret these findings to the courts.

These are the kinds of questions expert witnesses involved in sexual harassment cases might be asked:

1. What is meant by sexual harassment, and how do you define this?
2. What are some common examples of sexual harassment?
3. How does sexual harassment affect an individual?
4. In your opinion, how might sexual harassment affect an individual's performance on the job?

Competency

Although competency is traditionally an area dominated by clinical psychologists and psychiatrists, the opinion regarding an individual's capacity to stand trial or accept responsibility for his or her acts is increasingly opening to properly trained and credentialed counselors. Some states still specify via statute (law) that this role may be reserved for certain disciplines. It is advisable to be aware of your state's regulation in this area before offering or consenting to serve in this role. A strong background in the use of diagnostic instruments and clinical interviews is necessary for those seeking work in this area, as is the appropriate state license or national certification. Traditionally, competency hearings centered around criminal actions as the courts attempted to determine a person's "sanity" (a legal concept), the person's responsibility for his or her actions, or the person's ability to stand trial. Competency questions may now arise in certain custodial or civil cases and can include the effects of substance or alcohol abuse as well as an individual's mental or psychological status. The consultant may be called upon to interview and test a client, or may testify based on others' findings. Perhaps the Jeffrey Dahmer murder trial in Milwaukee is a good example of how well-qualified experts may have varying opinions of the same individual. In this gruesome trial, experts had differing opinions regarding Dahmer's sanity and responsibility for his actions.

These are the kinds of questions expert witnesses involved in competency cases might be asked:

1. In your opinion, could an individual with an IQ similar to the client's understand the questions being posed to him or her?
2. Based on your interview and the testing that you have performed, have you arrived at a diagnosis for this client?
3. How might an individual that has been diagnosed as suffering from (for example) a major affective disorder be expected to react in this situation?
4. Do you believe that the client was aware of his or her actions at the time of the alleged incident?

Negligence/Malpractice

Unfortunately, not all health care professionals always act in the best interests of their clients or patients. In such instances, it may be alleged that a professional did not follow accepted methods of practice in treatment. Criminal or civil, or both, types of actions may be taken by a plaintiff. Counselors may be called upon to comment upon the treatment practices of other counselors or allied mental health providers. They may also be called upon to comment on the developmental, psychological, or vocational implications of alleged malpractice by any professional.

These are the kinds of questions expert witnesses involved in negligence/malpractice cases might be asked:

1. What is the accepted treatment in your field for a client experiencing (for example) chronic anxiety?
2. What does your professional code of ethics say regarding dual relationships?
3. Are you aware of any research or studies that have been done that discuss the potential harm in counselor-client sexual relationships?
4. Assuming that counselor Jones behaved in such a manner as I have described to you here today, in your opinion has he or she followed accepted practice in behaving in this manner?

Pain and Suffering

Because some counselors have expertise in the nonmedical treatment of chronic pain or the effects of pain upon physical, psychological, or vocational functioning, they are being called as expert witnesses in this area. Through test data and interviews, they help the courts determine the effects of an individual's pain, or the individual's ability to function with varying degrees of pain, or the individual's ability to enjoy life as a result of chronic pain. In some cases, their testimony helps the court determine whether financial compensation for pain is to be awarded.

These are the kinds of questions expert witnesses involved in pain and suffering cases might be asked:

1. Have you had occasion in your practice and profession to deal with clients who are suffering from chronic pain?
2. In your opinion, what are the psychological effects of chronic pain?
3. From your perspective as a counselor, are there any accepted treatment procedures that you can use in dealing with pain?
4. Could an individual suffering from chronic pain as testified to by Mr. Jones and as reported by Dr. Smith, in her report of July 29, 1992, be expected to work at a competitive job on a sustained 40-hour-a-week basis?
5. In your opinion, can pain in and of itself be a disabling factor?

Addictions

Properly credentialed counselors are often called upon to discuss the effects of substance abuse and addiction on an individual's behavior and competency. The pervasive use of drugs and alcohol in our society unfortunately offers myriad opportunities for counselors with expertise in these areas to qualify as expert witnesses. This too was an area once dominated by medical specialists that, primarily due to increasing need, has now opened up for nonmedical practitioners.

These are the kinds of questions expert witnesses involved in addiction cases might be asked:

1. In your practice and previous experience, have you had occasion to work with individuals who have used the drug known as (for example) crack?
2. Have you worked with individuals who have chronically abused alcohol? In your opinion, can alcohol be addicting?
3. Are you aware of any common behavioral manifestations of an individual who has recently used (for example) cocaine?
4. Are there interventions or treatment programs that are known to be effective in dealing with (for example) alcohol addiction?

Summary

You can expect to be approached to serve as an expert witness in any area in which you are qualified to formulate a professional opinion. Be prepared by keeping abreast of the latest developments in your field. Read your journals and stay current in your field. Even those not in private practice are finding increasing opportunity or employer pressure to serve in the capacity of expert witness.

Relationships With Parties Being Evaluated

Technically, the attorney or agency who retains you is your client. However, in this chapter, we are talking about the relationship the expert witness has with the person being evaluated. We use the terms *subject* to refer to the person whom you are evaluating or discussing and *attorney* or *retaining attorney* for the person who hired you. In most instances in which you have been retained as an expert, the retaining attorney (or agency) asks you what specific reports and documents are necessary for you to reach an opinion. These are usually provided to you directly by the attorney or agency with no contact between you and other professionals who may be involved in the case.

In many instances, you are allowed to interview and test the subject involved in the action that is pending. Here you must remember that your role is as an evaluating (versus treating) professional. Because you have been retained to give an opinion regarding your findings, there are some major differences in how you approach the subject to be interviewed. You must make it clear to the subject that confidentiality or privileged communication does not apply between you and him or her, that you have been retained by a certain party to evaluate or interview him or her for a specific purpose. You should also make it clear to the subject that you are likely to be called upon to testify (and on whose behalf) as to your opinions via report or deposition, or in open court.

We recommend making a statement such as the following:

> Mr. Jones, my name is Dr. Weikel. I'm not a medical doctor, but a counselor who specializes in vocational matters (or rehabilitation etc.). I've been retained by your attorney, Ms. Jane Smith, to evaluate your vocational potential in light of your injuries and offer an opinion regarding your ability to work and whether or not you've suffered any degree of occupational disability. I'll be asking you some questions about your injury and how it affects you and your ability to function, that is, about what you can and cannot do. Next, I'll ask about your education, any training you have had, and the work that you have done in the past as well as any plans you may have for future training or work. I'll also be administering some tests to help me render an opinion in your case. When I finish the interview, I'll be studying the reports from your medical doctors. After I've done all of this, I'll submit a written report to your attorney. If she feels my findings will help your case, she will probably take my deposition or ask me to appear in person at your trial. Do you have any questions before we begin?

After studying a case or interviewing a subject, you may find it necessary to request additional information regarding that person. You should ask the attorney who retained you to provide such information or to schedule other consultative examinations as you feel necessary. In all cases, your request should be made directly to the attorney who retained you since that person is responsible (financially and otherwise) for directing the progress of the case.

Next, you must remember that, in your role as an expert, you have limited face-to-face contact with a subject that you may be evaluating. Avoid providing treatment or criticizing another's treatment based on hearsay report. Defer or refer a subject's questions to a treating professional, and be careful not to go beyond your area of acknowledged expertise.

Remember that anything you generate in terms of test data and notes regarding a client is likely to be viewed by opposing counsel and might possibly become an exhibit (evidence) in the case. The argument that notes are work products usually only prevents an attorney from sharing his or her notes and in most cases does not apply to materials you, as a witness, generate in reaching your conclusions. Therefore, you must be careful what you write regarding any client. Be prepared to back up your opinion and assertions based on the evidence of record and your own findings. Diagnoses should be based primarily on objective clinical evidence.

Study all relevant evidence well. Use medical, psychological, educational, and vocational reports as a solid foundation for your opinions. Be prepared to testify as to how varying (and often conflicting) medical and psychological reports affect your opinion. Your job is not to decide which report or opinion is correct but to respond hypothetically to these reports, assuming that each in turn is factual. The courts—judges, juries, or hearing officers—are the deciders of fact. Your task is to help them reach an informed decision. Remember, you are not a client advocate when you perform the duties of an expert witness but rather an objective witness who "teaches" the court through your learned opinions. You should have no concern or interest in the outcome of a case. Your testimony is usually only one small part of the overall evidence presented. You offer a fair and unbiased opinion and then go on to the next case.

The Attorney's Role

The plaintiff is the individual or entity who has initiated the litigation, whether it be a Workers' Compensation claim, a Social Security claim, a divorce action, or a negligence claim. The defendant is the individual or entity who has been charged with being responsible for the damage the plaintiff has suffered (that is, the service provider, the person driving the car that hit the plaintiff, or the employer of the employee who was hurt at work). Each party has the right to be represented by counsel. It is the attorney, not the client, who most is likely to contact you to give an expert opinion.

Attorneys should take every step possible within their physical and financial means to represent the interests of their clients. This duty is one of the reasons the attorney seeks an expert's opinion. In addition, the expert's opinion is an effective settlement tool against opposing counsel or a client with unreasonable expectations. For example, the attorney-author of this monograph has used an expert's opinion in convincing her own client that his demands for total disability were unreasonable in a Workers' Compensation claim when the vocational expert stated that the client's occupational disability was only 25%.

The role of the attorney using an expert is not only to enlighten the judge or jury but also to convince them that the expert's opinion is correct. Once the attorney has inquired as to the expert's opinion based upon assumed facts, the expert states that opinion, and the attorney and expert enter into a contract. The expert, by view of his or her opinion, then becomes a de facto advocate for the client. The opposing attorney (and the jury) know that you are being compensated for your time. Be wary of queries like "How much were you paid for your opinion?" or "How much did Mr. Smith pay you to tell the jury that the plaintiff couldn't work anymore?" Simply respond that you are compensated by the hour or by the case, whatever your method of charge is, and emphatically stress that you are not being paid just to express a favorable position.

The judge at trial or a hearing officer at an administrative proceeding presides over the hearing. He or she determines what evidence is admissible and what is not admissible. You should be aware that the opposing attorney may object to different statements of your testimony. The most common objection concerning expert testimony is that you are not a qualified expert on the subject matter. The judge determines whether or not the expert is qualified. Before the judge can make this determination, the attorney who hired you attempts to qualify you by asking several questions. For example:

1. Tell the jury your name.
2. What is your occupation?
3. What is your professional address?
4. Tell the jury about your education.
5. Are you a member of any professional organizations or societies?
6. Have you written any publications or articles in your field?
7. Approximately how many times have you testified and given expert opinion in matters such as this?

The opposing attorney may object when the expert begins to give his or her opinion by claiming that there is no foundation for the opinion. The judge determines whether or not a proper foundation for the opinion has been laid. Simply speaking, think of the expert's opinion as a completed brick house. Each brick is a question and answer providing the foundation for the opinion. An example of a proper foundation for a rehabilitation counselor giving an opinion as a vocational expert as to occupational disability is as follows:

- Doctor, did you evaluate a Ms. Mary Smith on July 1, 1992, at my request, for the purpose of giving an opinion as to her occupational disability?
- What medical reports were provided to you concerning Ms. Smith?
- What work, medical, and personal history did you obtain from Ms. Smith?
- What tests did you administer to Ms. Smith?
- What were the results of those tests?
- What did Ms. Smith state were her current physical complaints?
- Based on the medical reports that you have received, the tests that you have administered, and the personal history that you have taken from Ms. Smith, can she, in your opinion, return to her customary work?
- Based on the above factors, in your opinion, has Ms. Smith suffered any degree of occupational disability? If so, what is the percentage of occupational disability?
- Doctor, have all of your answers here today been given with a reasonable degree of certainty within your field?

In cases where a jury is present, its members decide the outcome based on the facts presented to them. The expert should speak to the jury in answer to the attorney's questions and make eye contact with the jurors. If reference is made to charts or other documents, explain them clearly and in lay terms so that the jury understands what you are trying to tell them.

Rules of Evidence

Most jurisdictions have codified rules of evidence that govern the procedure by which an attorney must prove a case. For example, a client who worked as a hospital orderly tells the attorney that he or she received a back injury while lifting a 300-pound patient. Immediately, the attorney knows the injury has given rise to a Workers' Compensation claim. How can the attorney prove this to the Workers' Compensation Board? The rules of evidence that govern civil cases and specific rules that govern compensation cases tell the attorney the method he or she must use.

We have all watched enough lawyer shows on television to know that the most common form of evidence is the testimony of a witness. The claimant (plaintiff) and individuals who saw the injury occur are called, either by deposition or to appear live at a hearing, to testify or tell the hearing officer what they saw happen.

The next most commonly used type of evidence is the testimony of an expert witness. In this example, experts commonly used include the medical doctors and chiropractors who treated the claimant and counselors giving vocational testimony as to the subject's occupational disability. Other forms of evidence are the written medical reports concerning the treatment the patient has undergone and a written vocational report by the counselor.

In most administrative proceedings, the depositions can actually be submitted as proof in the case, and the expert witness does not need to testify at the hearing in person. In the past few years, it has become an accepted practice to offer an expert's testimony by video deposition in actual trials. In the past, the only method to introduce the opinion of an expert who was unavailable for trial was to have someone play the role of the expert, reading the actual expert's answers from a previous deposition in response to the attorney's previously asked questions. Although this is still allowed in most jurisdictions, it is an ineffective method because it tends to bore both judges and juries.

At trial, most attorneys prefer to have the expert present to testify live. However, this is not always possible due to scheduling problems, previous commitments on the expert's part, delays at trial, and the economic cost to the attorney's client. For the attorney, it does not make sense to have the expert sitting at the courthouse with the "meter running" because the attorney is unable (through no fault of his or her own) to anticipate the exact time the expert will be called to testify. Thus, more and more attorneys are utilizing the video deposition method of taking expert testimony, which is then played in court on a regular video-cassette recorder and television. The jury is admonished by the judge to give this type of testimony the same weight as if the expert were testifying in person.

Always ask the attorney who is scheduling your deposition if it is by video. As a counselor and expert witness, appropriate dress is required.

The Discovery Process

Before you testify, it is imperative that you have a basic understanding of the discovery process. This is the time period after the action has been filed and prior to the hearing or trial date. Depending upon the type of litigation involved, the time periods vary. In some jurisdictions, economic litigation rules apply that serve to accelerate the discovery time periods. Always ask the attorney seeking your opinion about the time frame in which you are working. All competent attorneys keep a working calendar with the discovery deadlines clearly marked.

During the discovery period, the parties are allowed to send written questions, called interrogatories, to the other parties. In addition to discovering the basis of the opposing party's claim or defense, attorneys commonly use this discovery tool to find out which experts have been consulted and retained by the opposing counsel.

If asked, the opposing party must disclose which experts have been consulted but were not hired. All attorneys should want to know why an expert who was consulted was not employed. This too can serve as an excellent reference source of experts for an attorney.

Finally, most jurisdictions require the attorney to disclose not only the expert's identity but also the subject matter upon which the expert will be testifying; the substance of the facts and opinion to which the expert is expected to testify; and a summary of the grounds for each opinion. Because of these requirements, the attorney needs to know what your opinion is and the basis for your conclusions.

A word of caution to the potential expert: Be careful of what you write to the attorney who has retained your services. Opposing attorneys love to hang experts with their own words. Base your opinions only on the facts presented to you.

Without question, the most commonly used discovery tool of any attorney is the deposition. As an expert witness, you can expect to spend a significant amount of time giving discovery and other depositions.

Preparing to Testify and Giving Testimony

After you have studied a case and perhaps met with or evaluated a subject, you are usually asked to submit a written report to the retaining attorney. Carefully prepare the report, making sure that your findings are solidly rooted in the evidence or in data obtained from your interview. When the retaining attorney receives your report, he or she decides if your findings help the case to the point that it warrants further expenditure of funds. If your report harms the case or adds little, your involvement may cease at this point, and you need only submit your bill for payment. In most instances, opposing counsel is provided with your report, or demands to see a copy, because attorneys are required to share their lists of those experts who they plan to call upon early in the litigation process. The opposing attorneys may then decide that your findings strengthen their case. If so, they may take your deposition to get your report into evidence, and they are liable for your fees from this point. Opposing attorneys may also demand to take your deposition for discovery purposes, which is well within their rights, and in this case, they are usually responsible for the deposition fee. However, it doesn't hurt to ask to whom the bill should be sent prior to the deposition.

In most cases that may eventually go to court or to a hearing, the attorney or party who retained you will request a deposition time and date, and should accommodate your professional schedule. Allow enough time for a meeting with the attorney who retained you prior to the deposition. Because attorneys don't like asking witnesses questions unless they know how the witness will respond, expect a "dry run" of the questioning at this meeting. This will also prepare you for the actual questioning. Unfortunately, you don't get to have such a trial run with opposing counsel, so you need to be well prepared and anticipate questioning on cross-examination! The retaining attorney may be able to help you to anticipate the types of questions the opposing counsel may ask. In our experience, most depositions run anywhere from about 20 minutes to 2 hours, but on rare occasions they can run considerably longer. Until you get a feel for an average time for your depositions, schedule at least 2 hours before your next appointment. In a predeposition meeting, the retaining attorney may discuss many aspects of the case as well as his or her strategy in the case. With experience, you will be able to help attorneys make the best use of your testimony by helping them to frame questions or to emphasize certain of your findings. If you have previously given a deposition for discovery or other purposes in this case, request a copy and read it so that you are consistent in your responding. Experts who contradict themselves or are unsure or wishy-washy find very little repeat business because their testimony is supposed to be based on assumed facts. It is a safe practice to expect your deposition to be taken in every case. It is also true that live trial appearances have decreased due to video depositions and the fact that most cases settle before an actual trial.

What to Expect

The rituals of trials, administrative hearings, and depositions are fairly similar, with trials perhaps more formal than depositions. In trials, you can expect a judge, complete with robes and gavel and perhaps even a jury. The proceedings take place in a federal, state, or county courthouse that typically has all of the trappings of a television courtroom. Most likely, a bailiff is present and calls you into the courtroom when it is your turn to testify. Microphones to amplify your voice and additional microphones for recording your testimony are commonly found on the witness stand. Many witness boxes have a shelf or table where you can lay out your notes and papers, but some simply have a chair. If possible, check out the courtroom prior to giving testimony because you may need a briefcase to serve as a lap table. In administrative hearings, expect either a hearing officer or administrative law judge but no jury because the hearing officer is the decider of fact. The officer may or may not wear robes, and the location can vary from a semiformal hearing room to an informal office or even a hotel room for a traveling administrative law judge. Expect a recording device and either a court reporter or hearing assistant, but less formality than in the actual courtroom. In depositions, there is no judge or hearing officer. You give a sworn statement to be used at a later time or give information for the purpose of discovery to the opposing counsel. Frequently, your deposition is taken in lieu of your appearance at trial. It is read into evidence as if you were there in person and testified to the same. In other instances, a video deposition is taken, and the judge or jury views you on video as if you had been present to testify in person. For depositions, expect only a court reporter or camera technician. Depositions are typically taken in your office for your convenience.

In all cases, you begin by being sworn. You are asked to raise your right hand and to swear by oath to tell the truth. If you have a religious objection to taking an oath, you may affirm, under the penalty of perjury, to tell the truth. Once you have been sworn, the questioning begins. Usually, except in discovery depositions, the attorney who employed you begins by examining your qualifications to serve as an expert. Opposing counsel may voir dire and then object to you as an expert. The voir dire process allows the opposing attorney to question any perceived weakness in your educational background, training, and experience. He or she may use this opportunity to introduce doubt into the jury members' minds regarding your expert status. Remember that you have no control over this process and are bound to give accurate answers to each question, without appearing defensive. More likely, the opposing counsel stipulates your qualifications. By stipulating, he or she is simply agreeing that you are qualified to offer an opinion, but not that he or she necessarily agrees with that opinion. The opposing attorney may often stipulate the expert's credentials so that the jury won't hear this long list of impressive qualifications.

Next, the direct questioning begins. You are asked to review your findings and give an opinion on the matter at hand. Be prepared to discuss how you arrived at your conclusions and be able to lay a strong foundation for any opinion that you give. By this we mean that you must be able to respond to the facts in evidence in the case or to your own objective findings in rendering an opinion. You may be asked to cite or to produce any documents that you relied upon in reaching an opinion. You may also have to produce any tests or other instruments that were used.

If during the proceedings (deposition or trial) an attorney objects to a question or to your response, stop talking. In trials, the judge instructs you whether or not to answer a question following an objection. In instances of depositions for which there is no judge, the attorney who retained you tells you when to answer.

Expect an in-depth cross-examination to follow direct questioning. Remember, the job of the opposing counsel is to discredit or poke holes in your testimony or to inject doubt regarding your findings. This is not and should not be seen as a personal attack, but rather a challenge of your findings as the opposing attorney tries to protect the interests of his or her client. Following cross-examination, there may be a re-direct line of questioning and then a re-cross. In direct examination, the attorney who retained you tries to introduce your findings that are favorable to his or her case clearly into evidence. In cross-examination, opposing counsel tries to hit upon the perceived weak points and damage or discredit your testimony and perhaps inject doubt upon your findings and opinions. If your retaining attorney thinks this has happened, he or she goes back to re-direct questioning to try to repair whatever damage the opposing counsel has done to your testimony, at which point opposing counsel may re-cross. Re-direct and re-cross may continue until both sides are finished questioning and feel that they have made their points. At this time the deposition ends, or, if in court, you may leave the witness stand. The judge usually informs you that you are excused. If in doubt, ask the judge, "Am I free to leave?" or "Am I excused?" In most cases where you testify, you never know the outcome of the case. Your involvement ceases at this point, but you should save your records (up to about 2 years) in case of a mistrial, appeal, or further proceedings, in which case you may be recalled to testify.

Some Do's and Don't's

Remember that you have been called upon as an expert based on your knowledge or skills to help a judge, hearing officer, or jury make an informed decision. You have usually been retained by one of two opposing sides because they feel that your testimony strengthens their case. Prepare well! Study all relevant evidence carefully to reach your conclusion. Be able to justify your findings based on scientific fact, your knowledge in the field, or your evaluation of a subject. Be versed on the strengths and weaknesses of any instruments that you rely upon in your evaluations. Experienced cross-examiners may ask about things such as validity, reliability, and standard error of measurement; but remember, you are the expert in your field! When you arrive at a court trial, never enter the room until called by the bailiff. In some circumstances, this could be the grounds for a mistrial because witnesses generally are not allowed to hear the testimony of prior witnesses. Check with the attorney who retained you about the location of the witness room or about where you should wait to be called. In addition, avoid all contact and conversation with jurors during breaks or recesses.

Listen carefully to questions as they are posed to you. Answer concisely without volunteering additional information. Avoid jargon and use language that laypeople can understand rather than trying to baffle or impress them. Avoid "iffy" answers. If you can't answer a question, say so. You will find that your best sources of new referrals are a result of your performance in the present case. Every new opposing attorney becomes a potential referral source.

Be professional. You are representing your profession as well as yourself. Dress appropriately. Speak slowly and carefully and think before you talk. Refer to your notes. Don't try to impress others with your memory. Above all, take the high ground relating to ethics. Be objective and unimpeachable in your testimony. Basically your job is very simple. All you have to do is to tell the truth as you see it.

Frequently Asked Questions

Q. What licenses or certificates do I need to serve as an expert witness?

A. There is no license, certificate, or particular credential necessary to serve as an expert witness. However, as a mental health professional, you should possess all appropriate state licenses (if available) and national certificates in your field before offering your services as an expert. Expert status is conferred by the courts via the presiding judge on a case-by-case basis. You might have an ongoing contract with an agency or court system to serve as an expert when needed.

Q. I have been asked to serve as an expert witness by a local attorney. How much should I charge for my services?

A. Fees should be set on a per-hour basis for services rendered and should be in line with the prevailing rate charged by other mental health professionals in your geographic area. Depositions and court appearances are usually billed at two to four times the hourly rate to compensate for preparation and travel. Your rates should be consistent regardless of which side retains you, and they should never be contingent on the outcome of a case.

Q. I administered a restricted, copyrighted psychological test to a client. Now the opposing attorney wants to make the actual test an exhibit in the case, by attaching it to my deposition. What should I do?

A. Protest mildly regarding the confidential nature of this restricted and copyrighted material and then request that if the judge rules to admit it as evidence, it be sealed evidence and not subject to public scrutiny after the trial has ended. You are obliged to provide all materials used in reaching your conclusions and may not withhold any potential evidence by claiming privileged communication when you are functioning as an expert witness. The presiding judge rules as to what is admissible as evidence. You are not liable to any action or in violation of your ethical code when you are following the directive of a presiding judge. To do otherwise could expose you to being in contempt of court.

Q. I have been asked to serve as an expert witness in a case against another counselor. Should I do this?

A. Yes! You will not be the one to decide whether a peer committed malpractice, but your objective testimony can help the court to decide. You may be asked to elaborate on standard practice and procedure, but others decide if your peer deviated in a harmful way from these practices. A profession has an obligation not only to police itself through ethical boards but also to protect the public from errant members. By offering your services, you might help to right a potential wrong or to clear the name of one who has been wrongly accused.

Q. Do I need a doctorate to become an expert witness?

A. No. The majority of counselors practice at the master's level, so a master's degree is acceptable. Keep in mind, however, that the courts confer expert status regardless of educational level and that the ultimate decision about any person's qualifications rests with the presiding judge. Obviously, the better your credentials, the fewer challenges you might expect to your expert status. If you are challenged as an expert and a judge determines you are not qualified, do not be offended or in any way try to argue. Prepare for challenges to your credentials, but always accept a judge's decision.

Q. What if I am evaluating a person for expert witness purposes and the subject wants to talk to me confidentially?

A. You must make it clear to people you see in this capacity that confidentiality does not apply. They should know who retained you and for what purpose. They should also realize that your findings will be used to help you to reach an opinion in their case and will be shared with the parties involved, possibly in open court. A signed document indicating that the client understands the relationship is preferable.

Q. I appeared as an expert witness in a court case, and the opposing attorney was mean and rude to me on cross-examination. What should I have done?

A. Nothing. Although the attorney may have lacked grace and manners, he or she was most likely trying to do his or her job. The opposing attorney, in general, wants to discredit your testimony, question your credentials, or introduce doubt or uncertainty. Maintain you cool and don't die on the cross (examination). Testifying in a convincing manner is what you are being retained to do. If the attorney who retained you feels you are being badgered or treated unfairly, it is his or her job to object. Remember not to take challenges, attacks, or sarcasm personally. It comes with the territory.

Guidelines for Practice

If you are asked to serve as an expert witness...

1. Do you have the knowledge and expertise in your field necessary to do the job?
2. Can you "teach" or convey this knowledge to a judge, hearing officer, or jury?
3. Can you make the commitment of time necessary to do an adequate job?
4. Do you understand the differences in role between a counselor and evaluator or expert witness?
5. Can you take the stress or pressure that can accompany the duties of an expert witness?

When meeting with a subject for evaluation prior to providing expert witness testimony...

1. Make it clear to the subject that confidentiality does not apply. A signed release form is recommended.
2. Follow accepted practice and procedures.
3. Take detailed notes.
4. Prepare a comprehensive written report outlining your findings and opinions.
5. Base your opinions on facts.

When preparing for a deposition, hearing, or court appearance...

1. Review your notes and other materials.
2. Make sure that your file includes all documents and tests related to the case.
3. Have a clear copy of your report, including your findings and opinions.
4. Meet with the attorney who retained you for a dry run of anticipated questioning.

When appearing for a deposition, hearing, or court appearance...

1. Dress appropriately as a member of your profession.
2. Bring your entire file with all references, tests, notes, and relevant reports.
3. Refer to your notes throughout the questioning. Don't rely on your memory.
4. Answer in a clear and concise manner. Do not volunteer information or ramble.
5. If a jury is present, make eye contact when appropriate with the jurors.
6. Listen to the judge or hearing officer and do as he or she directs.
7. If you are unsure of a question, ask the person to repeat or rephrase the question.
8. Stay calm and always tell the truth!

Summary

Is it worth the time and effort on your part to become a knowledgeable expert witness? In our opinion, the answer is "Yes." This country was formed on a principle of equal justice for all. By serving as an expert, you can help judges, hearing officers, or juries see that all persons receive a fair hearing and that informed decisions are made. It is not a perfect world out there! There are dishonest people who try to "beat the system" in all walks of life. You can help to make a difference by learning to express your professional opinion in an honest and professional manner. Experienced attorneys recognize the benefits of expert testimony in educating a judge or jury and in helping them make informed decisions. As a client advocate, the attorney calls upon all necessary resources to present the best case for his or her client.

For you as a counselor there are many benefits in becoming an expert. First, it is a significant source of income to supplement your practice or other wages. It can help you to become more visible in your community and put you in contact with many other professionals who are potential referral sources. By learning a new role as expert witness, you can more fully understand how the unique relationship you have with your counseling clients differs from the role you take as an evaluator and witness. The evaluating experience also serves to broaden your experience with various types of clients, perhaps not seen in your routine practice. Virtually every community has a need for expert witnesses in a variety of actions. By qualifying and agreeing to serve, you are providing a service to your community and helping to advance your profession.

We believe in the skills possessed by professional counselors, and we believe that counselors can and do have unique training that can be of benefit to the larger community. By serving as an expert, you take your skills from behind the closed door of the treatment room and allow others to see the myriad talents possessed by today's new breed of counselor. In the process, you also help to strengthen our country's legal system and to ensure justice for all.

Discussion Questions

1. What is an expert witness? How does the role of expert witness differ from the traditional counselor's role? How does a counselor serving as an expert witness deal with confidentiality?

2. Who employs an expert witness? How do I qualify to serve as an expert? What education, training, and credentials do I need? How can I get started? What should I charge? In what types of actions can counselors appear as experts?

3. Because I'm the expert in my field, why doesn't the judge or jury simply ask me for my opinion or recommendation and follow it? Why can a noncounselor, that is, an attorney, attack my credentials or opinions? Why all the formality in this process?

4. Should I only take cases for plaintiffs since I was trained to be a client advocate? If the defendant is a big insurance company, can I charge them more than if I were working for a plaintiff? Because depositions are time consuming and stressful, can I charge more than my normal hourly rate? Can I be hired directly through the courts?

5. The attorney who retained me asked a question, and the other attorney objected. Should I answer? Why do they want to

know about my degrees, publications, and credentials? Do I have to discuss all of my income from various sources? How long can they keep asking these questions? If I don't know the answer to a question, should I fake it?

Suggested Readings

Blau, T. (1984). *The psychologist as expert witness.* New York: Wiley & Sons. The early "bible" for counselors serving as expert witnesses. Although written primarily for clinical psychologists, it is a very useful book in explaining the role of the expert witness and offering advice on how to best serve in this capacity.

Remley, T. P., Jr. (1991). *Preparing for court appearances.* AACD Legal Series, Vol. 1. Alexandria, VA: American Association for Counseling and Development. This monograph discusses counselors in court, the adversarial system, subpoenas, consulting with attorneys, and general witness versus expert witness testimony.

Remley, T. P. Jr., & Miranti, J. (1991). Child custody evaluator: A new role for mental health counselors. *Journal of Mental Health Counseling, 13*(3), 334–342. An in-depth look at the role of the mental health counselor as an impartial child custody evaluator for the courts. Included are sections on the evaluation process, the evaluation report, and testifying in court.

Weikel, W. J. (1986). The expanding role of the counselor as vocational expert witness. *Journal of Counseling and Development, 64*(8), 523–524. Discusses the role of vocational and rehabilitation counselors in evaluating clients for disability, Workers' Compensation, and personal injury. Included are tips on evaluation, witness behavior, and expanding a private practice by working within the legal system.

Wrightsman, L., Willis, C., & Kassin, S. (1987). *On the witness stand: Controversies in the courtroom.* Newbury Park, CA: Sage. Contains essays for mental health professionals on court testimony issues. A section on expert witnesses is included.

References

Gardner, R. (1982). *Family evaluation in child custody litigation.* Creskill, NJ: Creative Therapeutics.

Remley, T. P., Jr. (1991). *Preparing for court appearances.* AACD Legal Series, Vol. 1. Alexandria, VA: American Association for Counseling and Development.

Remley, T. P., Jr., & Miranti, J. (1991). Child custody evaluator: A new role for mental health counselors. *Journal of Mental Health Counseling, 13*(3), 334–342.

Weikel, W. J. (1986). The expanding role of the counselor as vocational expert witness. *Journal of Counseling and Development, 64*(8), 523–524.

Weikel, W. J., & Palmo, A. (1989). The evolution and practice of mental health counseling. *Journal of Mental Health Counseling, 11*, 7–25.

NOTES

NOTES

NOTES